How to Safely Use
The Ouija Board

By Daniel Cumerlato

© 2015 Daniel Cumerlato of The Ghost Walks
www.ghostwalks.com ~ All Rights Reserved

Table of Contents

Introduction – What is the Ouija Board? 3
   The History of the Planchette 3
   The History of the Ouija 5
   The Ouija Board as a Communication Tool 7
   Why should you use the Ouija Board? 9
   WARNING... The Bad Side of the Ouija 11
Instruction Manual ~ How to Safely use The Ouija Board 14
   The Big 3 Rules of Ouija 14
      Rule #1 - Be serious because it's not a game 14
      Rule #2 - Always say Goodbye 14
      Rule #3 - Never use the Ouija in your home 15
   Have Perfect Communication with the Dead 16
      The Team 16
      Details about each Role 18
      The Leader 18
      The Documenter 19
      The Energizer(s) 20
      How to Setup the Table 21
   How to talk to the dead 21
      What to know before Starting 22
      How to have a Great Session 23
      What to do when things go bad 28
   How to end the session 30
      Ghost Contact List 31
      Want to play again? 32
About the Author 33
Quick Instructions 34

Introduction – What is the Ouija Board?

The Ouija Board has been evil since 1973. Why 1973? That's the year The Exorcist was released into theatres, raising the horror genre to a new level and would forever demonize this once effective communication device.

That movie changed horror forever, and even today many are unable to watch it. This makes it easy to see why all of those "based on a true story" events would be feared.

What caused the demon to possess Regan in the movie? The dreaded Ouija Board did!

The History of the Planchette

The planchette is an upside-down heart shaped device that points to letters and numbers. This is where the Ouija began, through an ancient form of divination known as Automatic Writing.

Automatic Writing is the ability to channel spirit energy through a psychic person holding a pen and paper. The psychic person is believed to be controlled by ghost energy, as a way to pass messages to the living.

It would have been a great idea, if not for our natural human defenses. Even great psychics were unable to control the pen. Our living energy would fight the outside attack, causing results to be difficult or impossible to read, and thus ruining the communication.

Enter the ancient Chinese, and their method known as Fuji or "planchette writing". Who better than the most spiritual people on the planet to perfect this divination over 600 years ago?

A small wooden device can freely slide over a flat surface.

The Planchette solved two problems...

>#1 – Smooth and legible control of the pen
>#2 - Allowed many people to connect with the Planchette at one time

Allowing many people at once was an amazing discovery. For the first time a group could combine their energies for talking with the dead. This meant all us regular, non-psychic, people could match the high energy of a real psychic.

It would take 500 years for the next improvement to come along, when the world was introduced to the "talking board".

The History of the Ouija

The Talking Board was created by Elijah Bond and Charles Kennard, who began production in the United States in 1891. The ancient Planchette became the centerpiece of this board game. The pen and paper were gone, replaced by engrained letters and numbers on wood or cardboard.

The ownership of the Talking Board would change hands over the years, finally ending up on the desk of Mr. William Fuld. Fuld would successfully bring the idea to mainstream, and prove that mystery sells. Even gave the board a new name, calling it "Oui-ja" (from French and German words for "Yes").

The Ouija was popular, but Fuld was not. Much of his business life was filled with lawsuits and fights against those who tried to use the patented name for copycat games. The fight would continue up until Fuld's strange death in 1927.

Fuld was overseeing a flagpole replacement on the roof of his factory. The iron support he leaned against gave way and he fell backwards. There was nothing to grasp as he fell from the roof and hit the pavement so hard it broke his ribs, one shooting up through his heart. William Fuld died instantly.

How fitting his death would fit perfectly into the script of any horror movie.

His children continued the business until 1966 when toy manufacturer Parker Brothers bought the patent. They would sell the rights to Hasbro in 1991, who still produce the board today, sold in many toy stores as a board game.

The Ouija Board as a Communication Tool
Hasbro has forgotten one thing - the Ouija Board is not a game! Saying it sounds simple, but means everything. Seeing the Ouija as a communication tool (just like the Chinese did) removes much of the dark stigma associated with it.

I know this because for over 15 years I've personally been connected to the board. Before founding The Ghost Walks (www.ghostwalks.com), I was thrown into the world of ghosts because of the Ouija and a couple of powerful experiences.

How I got into ghosts…

I purchased a board from a garage sale in Hamilton, Ontario, Canada for $0.25. Over the next few months, my girlfriend and I would use it many times. We knew nothing, and the planchette was always very slow, communication difficult, and we would get impatient.

That would change at my parents' house. The session started slow and we quickly lost interest, but kept our hands on the Planchette. I started joking around. We were laughing at each other when Planchette took off, moving from letter to letter and spelling, "U R a happy couple". From that point on I was a believer.

A few months passed. We were living in Toronto and the same Ouija board was gathering dust in the cupboard. Until one uneventful night and we decided to try it again.

We setup a recorder and started with the simple question, "Spirit are you here?"

The planchette moved very slowly across the board up to "Yes". All our past frustrations returned, however we are Canadian and didn't want to be rude. The ghost eventually reached yes, and we ended the session.

Afterwards we listened to the recording. Our voices were clear in the distance, first me asking the question, and then right up against the microphone a strange, male voice whispered "Yes".

We slept with the lights on that night.

I've put my belief in the Ouija Board ever since, and it has become a staple of the Ghost Hunts.

The methods featured in this book are dedicated to that experience, gained from over 15 years of using this effective communication tool.

Why should you use the Ouija Board?

Talking to the dead is difficult for people who are not psychic. Even if you paid for a psychic reading, it's difficult to find true psychics as many are fakes.

Hasbro's marketing department may have never guessed it, but the Ouija Board would become the next big thing in ghost communication.

And for this reason, the Ouija <u>is not evil</u>, but instead an efficient way of mixing natural psychic ability in a controlled manner.

You don't believe me? Then let's compare other forms of communication:

- **Automatic Writing** –
  1 person that must be psychic
- **Channeling** –
  1 person that must be a great psychic
- **Séance** – Many people / 1 Psychic
  Must have a psychic to receive messages
- **Table-Tipping** – Many people / No Psychic
  Limited to Yes and No answers

And then we have…

- **The Ouija Board** – Many people / No Psychic
  Complete communication

It is the best form of ghost communication, perfected during a time when people were serious about spiritualism. Today's technology fails to address the powers of the mind and body, something that the Ouija Board answers with focused grace.

WARNING... The Bad Side of the Ouija
And now a disclaimer... The Ouija Board is a focal point of combined energy from a group of people. This creates a buildup, some of which can be negative.

The Exorcist movie got that right. Negative energy can easily build up and take over a session. Either from the ghosts who carry it, like chains behind Jacob Marley in A Christmas Carol, or from a person in the group who's had a stressful day.

But not to worry, you'll feel the session getting nasty. This happened to me while using the Ouija in a haunted shop...

> *There were three of us in the old shop on James Street South in Hamilton when we decided to contact the dead. Sitting at a small round table in the middle of the shop floor with our homemade Ouija Board, we set out to contact the resident ghost.*

Her name was Elizabeth, and she made herself known to multiple psychics. They said she didn't like us in her home and was causing negative energy to drive us away.

We wanted to learn more and knew the Ouija Board was our best bet.

The old woman eventually came through. We asked, "Do you want us to leave?", and the planchette stopped. The board didn't respond, however the room did.

We started feeling very strange, like the air was heavy and hard to breath. Something was watching us from the empty psychic parlour, from the backroom, and in every dark corner.

The feeling of dread was so uncomfortable we decided to end the session by forcing the Planchette to 'Goodbye' and quickly leaving.

The next day the shop felt normal again.

This was my first lesson in how negative energy can easily affect the living. Not like a violent horror movie, but more in an emotional way, which can sometimes be worse than physical pain.

Keep this in mind as you now learn how to contact the dead.

Instruction Manual ~
How to Safely use The Ouija Board

The Big 3 Rules of Ouija

There are 3 main rules for a safe and effective session...

#1 – Be serious because it's not a game

#2 – Always say "Goodbye" at the end of the session

#3 – Never use the Ouija Board in your home

Rule #1 - Be serious because it's not a game

Being in a serious mood ensures your natural psychic defenses are switched on while you're talking to the dead. You are ready for negative energy, naturally closing yourself off to it, and protecting yourself from it.

Rule #2 - Always say Goodbye

Mischievous or negative ghosts will refuse to say Goodbye. This is like a stubborn child refusing to leave the store until you get them candy. You take the kid out of the store just like you put the planchette down to Goodbye. This ends the session and sets your mind, shutting the door from the other side.

Rule #3 - Never use the Ouija in your home

The negative energy from bad ghosts can affect you. You're at rest and want to feel comfortable in your home, a place where you're most vulnerable. The last thing you want is negative energy swirling about, affecting your mood, causing problems in your family, and nightmares while you sleep.

That's it, just 3 simple rules!

This is what everyone needs to know before using the board. It will act as your protector, giving the group one-mind and one-energy against anything that might come through the Ouija Board.

What about Rule #4 - Never use the Ouija alone?
There is no rule #4 for two main reasons...

First, people who are not psychic (most of us) don't have the energy to create sessions when alone. Psychics with high energy are able to control it.

Second, the best communication, and the reason the Ouija was invented, is for the combined energy of a group. Without the group, little to nothing will happen.

Have Perfect Communication with the Dead

The 3 elements of a great Ouija Board session are...

1. The Team
2. Methods for Talking to the Dead
3. Ending the session correctly

Here's what you'll need to start...

- ✓ 3-5 people
- ✓ A Ouija Board with Planchette
- ✓ Pen and Paper

The Team

Pick a group of 3 to 5 people and ensure they are all serious about talking to the dead. The class clown should stay home.

Do not have more than 5 people in the **Team** because many hands can be disruptive, and this causes too much energy.

Assign Roles to your Team

1. **The Leader**
   - 1 person who touches Planchette
   - Will control the session and lead communication

2. **The Documenter**
   - 1 person who doesn't touch Planchette
   - Will take notes and decipher what the ghost is trying to say

3. **The Energizer(s)**
   - 1-3 people who touch Planchette
   - Focused witnesses to lend energy but never talk

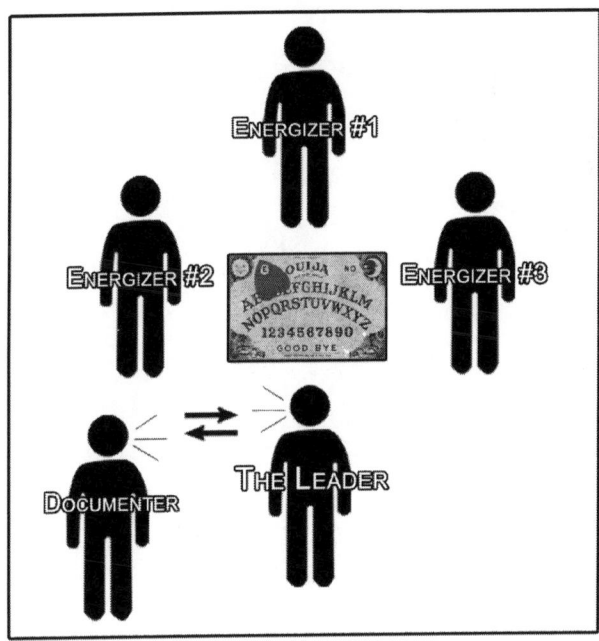

Details about each Role

Here are detailed descriptions of each role.

The Leader

1. **<u>Asks the questions</u>**

    Just like having a great conversation with a friend, it's important to ask the right questions. The **Leader** doesn't let the session get boring for you or the ghost.

    Here are some quick questions you could ask...
    a. The ghost's name
    b. The ghost's age when they died
    c. The ghost's gender
    d. What year did the ghost die in
    e. How did the ghost die
    f. Does the ghost have a message for someone in the room
    g. Is there anything the ghost wants from the group

2. **<u>Watches the Planchette and calls out the letters, numbers, Yes or No</u>**

    Since the **Leader** has the best view. Calls out for the **Documenter** to take notes. The **Leader** only calls out and never tries to understand until after the ghost is done each answer.

3. **Watch the session's energy**
   To confirm the session is energetic, if an **Energizer** is in a bad mood, or communication turns negative.

The **Leader** is beside the **Documenter**. After the ghost is done with the answer, the **Leader** can quietly converse with the **Documenter** to understand the communication.

The Documenter

The **Documenter** receives all communication by writing it down on paper. They can speak during the session, but should never ask questions directly to the ghost. Their questions should be whispered to the **Leader** so the **Leader** can ask.

The **Documenter** stays completely focused on understanding the communication.

When the **Leader** asks a question to the Ouija Board, the **Documenter** will…

1. **Write the question and answer as it happens**
   Write everything down before attempting to understand the communication.

2. **Understand then share**
   Always understand first and then share with the **Leader**. Talking out loud will only confuse everyone, including the ghost.
3. **Need more information from the ghost?**
   Sometimes the information is hard to understand or incomplete. Whisper any needed follow-up questions to the **Leader**, and the **Leader** will ask the ghost for you.

The Energizer(s)

Energizers are 1 to 3 people touching the planchette with the **Leader**. They don't speak or try to understand during the session. Their simple purpose is to lend energy.

A great **Energizer** can...

1. Stay still and focused
2. Be relaxed and flow with the Planchette's movement
3. Hear the **Leader's** question without assuming the answer

The **Energizer** will not fully understand any of the communication until the session is over and the team reviews everything. This is because they must remain so focused on the energy and movement of the planchette that everything else is lost.

How to Setup the Table

Use a square or rectangular table so...

1. The **Leader** and **Energizer(s)** can rest their arms.
2. The **Documenter** can easily sit beside the **Leader** for quiet communication.
3. The **Documenter** can have a good view of the board.

Put the Ouija Board directly in front of the **Leader** with the letters upright so they can easily read what the ghost is saying.

The **Leader** and **Energizer(s)** should be seated comfortably around the board, close enough to reach the Planchette without having to extend their arms, resting their elbows on the table.

The team and table are ready, now let's talk to the dead...

How to talk to the dead

Here are the main parts of a great Ouija Board session...

1. What to know before Starting
2. How to have a Great Session
3. What to do when Things go Bad

4. How to End the Session
5. How to Play Again

What to know before Starting

Here's what you need to know before starting the session...

1. **You want to communicate with the dead**
   Everything starts with this simple fact. Believing it creates positive reinforcement and a strong environment perfect for ghosts to enter.

2. **Avoid Interruptions for one hour**
   Make sure you have at least 1 hour of free, uninterrupted time for the session(s). During this time you can complete 1 to 2 active sessions, including review time.

3. **Turn off cell phones and devices**
   Distractions ruin results. This is a vintage form of spirit communication and all aspects of the session should remain vintage.

4. **What if my friends want to watch?**
   Only the team should be actively using the Ouija, however others can watch the session. Just make sure they are quiet, serious and focused.

5. **If the session slows or nothing is happening?**
   Switch roles on the team. New energies at different

roles will give different results. By changing roles you change the energy of the room.

6. **Do not assume!**
   What the ghost is saying might be obvious, but clear your mind and allow it to complete. Even if you ask a favorite color and it spells "W-H-I"... you know it's "White", but still allow the ghost to finish as not to confuse it.

Following the above creates focus that should turn to Ouija Board into an extension of the **Team's** arms and minds.

How to have a Great Session

Leader and **Documenter** listen up! This section is for you.

Study the following most common occurrences and you'll be ready for anything.

1. **Leader, here's how to move the planchette**
   Sometimes the planchette will start moving automatically when the team touches it. Other times your team will need patience and calm words of encouragement, as if trying to call over a scared pet.

What you might say...

"Spirit, this is a safe place. Please talk with us"

"Is there a spirit out there with a message for somebody at this table?"

"We'd like to call on the spirit of"... call someone personal or a previous connection

Get creative, but also remain calm and serious. Impatience and boredom are the quickest ways to end a session or attract a negative ghost.

2. **<u>What if the Planchette is unresponsive</u>**

    Oh no! The session is failing because the Planchette is slow or not moving at all.

    Time to <u>Switch Roles</u>...
    - Get the **Leader** to say Goodbye and end the session
    - Choose an **Energizer** to become the **Leader** and the **Leader** becomes an **Energizer**.
    - The **Documenter** can remain the same because their energy is not crucial.

    If the Planchette is still unresponsive, keep switching **Leaders** with **Energizers** until you run out of people in the **Team**. If there are spectators, start bringing them into the **Team**.

The session is over when you run out of people. Don't take it personally because some energies just don't mix.

3. **The infinity (figure 8) or circle movement**

    The infinity and circle are default movements for when energy is building up, or the session is transitioning from one ghost to another. It's a good thing because the Planchette is moving and energy is flowing. Don't fight it!

    The **Leader** can keep asking questions until the planchette responds again. Be happy because many teams can't even get the planchette to move.

4. **How to understand what the ghost is saying**

    Understanding messages can be a big challenge. Ghosts will often...
    - Speak in code
    - Misspell words (especially children)
    - Become confused if the team is not focused or two ghosts are fighting for control

Allow the spirit to finish talking even if the communication seems like gibberish. Often there are hidden messages for the **Documenter** to find.

If the same letters or numbers are being repeated more than twice, or the planchette stops, then the **Documenter** can begin understanding the message.

Be ready to have your time wasted because ghosts may be playing with you ion have all the time in the spirit world!

Here's how to best handle confusing messages…

1. **Sound it out** –
   if the spirit doesn't know how to spell
2. **Look for hidden words** –
   among the confusing letters
3. **Have the ghost repeat themselves** –
   say *"We didn't understand, please say that again"* This is very useful and gives the **Documenter** another chance to understand while maintaining high energy in the session.

5. **Read the emotion of the Planchette**
   It's not a romance novel, but a way of reading the

ghost's emotions through the movement of the Planchette.

A calm ghost
The Planchette will move slowly and slide easily around the board with clear stops and flowing communication. Little to no confusion.

A weak ghost
The Planchette will be slow, or fast and out-of-control. The stops are slightly away from letters and numbers. Communication may stop, or the Planchette will return to the middle of the board and "die" before randomly starting up again.

An upset or angry ghost
The Planchette will move fast. The team may find is difficult to keep their hands on the planchette as it whips around the board. This is the most exciting, and scary, of all Planchette emotions.

A spirit fight
This will cause sentences that don't make sense, erratic movements and constant stops. Happens when two energies try to communicate at the same time. The **Leader** can ask one of the

ghosts to move aside. If it doesn't stop, end the session and start over.

Over time you will learn how to naturally determine the emotion by movement and energy filling the room. If you have a psychic **Leader** or **Energizer**, they will be able to feel the emotion right away.

What to do when things go bad

Some ghosts are just bad, not "demon" bad, but negative or mischievous. Not once have I encountered something evil in over 15 years. Negative yes, demonic no!

So relax, because even the most negative ghost will never be dangerous. Still, it's best to deal with these bad energies as they happen. It might sound cool to have a bad ghost in your house, but it's not! This is where the Ouija's dark legends originate.

The negative energy can affect the emotions of you, your family and even your pets. It can cause marriages to break down, kids to be violent or even calm pets to become unsettled. All of it happening while you continue to wonder what the heck is going on.

How to know when it's a negative ghost

When a negative ghost enters the session, it'll be strong,

taking over the board quickly and moving the Planchette fast.

Communication is clear, but instead of positive information, you'll get insults, obscenities and threats. These bad ghosts will even threaten pain or death, which are empty threats but terrifying all the same.

You may start to feel uncomfortable or tense. It's similar to feelings of anxiety or nervousness. You'll be uneasy, your chest will be tight, the air around you becomes heavy and difficult to breath.

If it happens once...

1. Say Goodbye immediately
2. Take a break away from the board
3. Switch roles and start again

If it continues to happen...

1. Say Goodbye
2. Stop the session
3. End the night

After experiencing your first negative ghost, you'll fully understand why rule #3 (Never use the Ouija Board in your home) is so important.

How to end the session

The **Leader** says goodbye, the Planchette goes to the bottom and the **Leader** returns it to the middle of the board.

Now what?

1. The **Leader** must lift the Planchette off of the board and place it somewhere on the table, breaking the connection and releasing leftover energy.
2. The **Team** should leave the table and go to another location away from the Ouija before reviewing the session.
3. The **Documenter** goes over all communication with the **Team**.

While going over communication, <u>ask the questions</u>...

1. *Who was the ghost?*
2. *What were they trying to tell us?*
3. *Is there an important message for one of the* **Team** *members?*
4. *Do we want to talk with this ghost again?*

#4 is the most overlooked question. Haven't we all wanted a contact list of ghosts? Yes, the answer is definitely yes!

Ghost Contact List

This is something understood by every real psychic. Finding a positive spirit is like making a new friend ready to give advice whenever you want.

Once you have their name and can recognize their Planchette emotion, you can call on them during future sessions.

The **Documenter** should write down...

1. The ghost's name
2. How the Planchette is moving - fast, slow, erratic
3. Any unique characteristics, such as poor spelling or unique movement

How do you call on them?

Let's pretend the ghost is named Eric...

At the beginning of the session, the **Leader** says, *"We want to speak with our friend Eric. Please come through and talk with us. We are all your friends here."*

And when the planchette starts to move, make sure it matches the emotion and movement from last time, otherwise you could have a mischievous copycat ghost just looking for attention.

Want to play again?

How do we continue playing? Answer... Switch Roles!

You create new energy by...

1. Assigning a new **Leader**
2. Replacing **Team** members with spectators

Which will lead to different ghosts and energies coming through. Once shuffled, start a brand new session and continue talking to the dead.

When the night is over

When the night is all done, just clean up and put the Ouija Board away. You can safely store it anywhere because it's only a bundle of energy when in use.

End the night by promising always keep everyone's secrets. Personal information revealed by ghosts during sessions can strengthen a group of friends and make for a stronger **Team**.

Finding a great **Team** is rare, but once it happens never allow anything to come between you. These are now your life-long, and maybe even "after-death" friends.

About the Author

Daniel Cumerlato helped found the second oldest paranormal group in Canada over 15 years ago. Since then he's applied this extensive experience to The Ghost Walks (www.ghostwalks.com) - featuring tours and hunts in Hamilton & Niagara-on-the-Lake, Ontario, Canada.

Today, Daniel strongly holds on to the same dedication for the real world of ghosts, stories from believers, and constantly proving the world of the unknown.

He currently lives in the historic and haunted downtown of Hamilton, Ontario, Canada.

Quick Instructions

Be calm and spiritual by forgetting stresses and focusing on good.

The 3 Rules of using The Ouija Board

#1 – Be serious / #2 – Say "Goodbye" / #3 – Never use it at home

How to Talk to the Dead

Setup ~ Setup Ouija Board on square table in front of the Leader / Sit Documenter beside Leader and Energizer(s) near the Ouija

Important ~ Think "I want this" / At least one hour of free time / No cell phones / Spectators must focus and be calm / Switch Roles if unresponsive / Do not assume what will be said

Leader starts with "Spirit, this is a safe place"

Negative Spirit ~ Once, then end the session, take a break and try again / More than Once, then end for the night"

People / Roles

3 to 5 people - 1 Leader / 1 Documenter / 1-3 Energizers

Leader - On Planchette - Controls communication

Documenter - Not on Planchette - Notes, understands and assists

Energizers - On Planchette - Remain calm and focused

End the Session

Take planchette off board to break connection

Have team walk away, into another room if possible

Documenter goes over all communication with team...

Ask - *Who was the ghost? / What was the message? / Something specific for a team member? / Do we want to talk to this ghost again?*

Ghost Contact List - Document ghost's name and planchette emotion

Play again? - Switch roles and keep going

End of Night - Leave and never talk about your team's secrets!

Printed in Great Britain
by Amazon.co.uk, Ltd.,
Marston Gate.